SELECTED ART SONGS

OF

HELEN C. CRANE

MEDIUM VOICE

with piano accompaniment

BOOK ONE

Bernard R. Crane

Editor

ISBN 978-1-735-8882-7-9
BISAC: MUS037110
LOC Classification: M6 – 175.5

©2020 Bernard R. Crane
ASCAP

Helen C. Crane in her mid 20's (c. 1890)
enhanced photograph of Helen C. Crane as pictured in the publication
"The Music Monitor" July. 1919 – Vol. VIII, No. 10

DAYS OF DISCOVERY

Just a few minutes of spare time and a bit of curiosity is all that it took to launch myself on a quest that has now encompassed the last two years. Thanks to the wonders of the digital age more and more information is accumulated in smaller and smaller formats, occupying less and less space. Where once the entire floor of an office building was necessary to house one computer, now an entire library of reading material can be stored on a device not much larger than a little finger. One of the results of this every burgeoning ability to collect, store, and share materials is a unique collective enterprise known as International Music Score Library Project or IMSLP, present online at www.imslp.org . With the cooperation of individuals, schools and universities, through the pooling of resources we have reached a point where a significant portion of published music that is no longer copyright, is now available. In light of this rich source which I have used many times in the past, and being a composer myself, with degrees from Eastman and the San Francisco Conservatory, I was curious if there were any other CRANE's listed on IMSLP website. I did find five: Adam Crane, a gentleman who seems to have been more of a performer or teacher than a composer: his one page inclusion was "NiffTShift" some sort of performance method for shifting positions on a stringed instrument. Perhaps technically helpful, but artistically, not much. Frederick L. Crane: in some spots labeled "Fred L. Crane" - "After The Ball - a romance": having no relation to the old standard "gay nineties" tune; a brief piano piece, showy but with little integrity in the melodic line, harmony, in essence - blasé; J. W. Crane "2 Romances Sans Paroles": published in 1877 by Hartmann in Paris, very much "à la Mendelsohn or J. Burgmüller"; again, nice but not "earth-shaking". There was an entry for Lucy Crane, who apparently was sister of the noted illustrator Walter Crane, - her contribution is entitled "Baby's Opera"; (my thought on seeing the title, one might have difficulty holding the attention of either the cast, the audience or both.) Upon a closer look I see that it is a collection of nursery rhymes put to melody, which melodies she ascribed to "great masters of the past", so she is in fact the editor of the collection accompanied by artistic images of her brother, the noted illustrator. That leaves us with one remaining composer: Helen C. Crane and the "one" oeuvre that is listed here: her "Piano Trio in E Major, op.20". One piece, three movements, about 60 printed pages total, published in Germany by Gustav Vetter in 1907. I quickly ran off a copy, and waited anxiously for some spare time to run through it.

Eventually the opportunity came, one hour before a choral rehearsal which I was directing. When I began playing through the music I was actually amazed: it was quite bold, rather forward thinking; perhaps post-Brahms-ian, as one would hope, adventurous in its interrelation of keys, soaring melodies wonderful orchestration with each part very much in keeping with the technical parameters of each instrument. It seemed to be loaded with nuance, deeper meaning and ideas that warranted further study and repeated listening. There was certainly nothing wrong with any of the facets of the work, it showed great attention to detail, correct in all musical parameters on its face. I enjoyed the piece, beginning to end.

Opus 20 implied there had to be at least 19 other pieces or groupings of various sizes and instrumentation perhaps, but where were they? Were they ever published? What became of them? My mind was abuzz with curiosity and in the ensuing days I began some intensive exploration, running google searches and more, and it was not long before I came across an interesting discovery: in doing a search for "Helen C. Crane composer" I was ushered to a "url" which detailed a bequest from a New York City family to the city's library of all their important documents. This collection according to what I was able to ascertain was the Alexander Crane family's personal correspondence and spanned a period of more than a century, from the early 1800's to about 1940. Apparently Alexander was a personage of some note in New York City, enough so to warrant gathering together all of his correspondence in the NY Public Library. Closer examination showed that he was a Wall Street lawyer, a commissioned officer in the Civil War, and there was some sort of diplomatic connections in Italy,...why would this search for Helen Crane have brought me here?

Scanning through the contents of the collection which included a listing of family members, I came across Helen Cornelia Crane. Come to find out Helen C. Crane was Alexander's daughter and gradually the pieces began to fall into place. Helen's materials were not located with this larger collection at the main library. Rather her materials were housed at the NYPL "Cullman Center" Library for the Performing Arts at 40 Lincoln Center Plaza. When I checked this particular library's Helen C. Crane Collection listing, I was shocked! It was all there*; everything, either in its original manuscript form or both manuscript and published form along with ephemera concerning performances, playbills, requests from the Library of Congress for copies of awarded pieces, notes concerning her publishing agreements and records of payment, etc. a veritable mother-lode of material.

The only exception being her "Elegy for Cello" op. 57 for which she was awarded a prize in 1918. The Library of Congress subsequently requested a copy for their records (1944). Helen, having passed away in 1930, her sister, Caroline Crane Marsh obliged the Library of Congress, gifting them with what would seem to have been the only copy of the work. Hence, that work is no longer in the NYPL collection.

She was born in 1868 the second child with four sisters and a brother. She must have been very talented and showed a keen interest in the study of music. She ended up a student of Xaver Scharwenka, a noted Polish pianist and composer, who was performing and teaching from NYC at that time. Xaver's brother, Philip was also a musician, a pianist, composer, and educator and was director of the Klindworth-Scharwenka Conservatory in Berlin, Germany. I can only surmise that having worked with Ms. Crane, Scharwenka, became aware of her gifts and abilities and potential. With a brother heading up a conservatory in Europe, perhaps that would be the logical continuation of her studies, at this Berlin Conservatory with his brother as her composition teacher.

According to the NYPL Performance Library division whose listings I was able to find online, there were somewhere in the vicinity of 4 cu. ft. of original and published manuscripts of Helen's writings. The list included notations as to the nature of its contents, the various opus numbers, methods of copy, pen, pencil or published. It looked as though everything was there, however the breadth of her output was a bit larger than 20: there are 74 numbered works. ...op. 74 being her last. Included in her output were two symphonies with sketches for a 3rd, several symphonic tone-poems, well over 200 works for piano, choral works, songs for solo voice, sonatas for violin, cello, a larger work for orchestra and chorus. It was amazing.

I soon made my way to NYC to get a first hand look at this Collection that was locked away in the archives and only available by appointment. It was amazing to see the extent of the collection neatly housed in seventeen archival boxes. The documents were in pristine condition, bearing no impression they had been even touched since the day the were donated. The Library made no claims to copyright and certainly the pieces were past statutory protection (all except op.74 composed before 1923). They could not let the documents be photocopied but there was no prohibition on available-light images taken with a camera or cellphone. Over the next year with three successive visits to NY I came away with some 3,440 images of Helen's own manuscripts.

In sharing this music with others, people have asked the obvious question: "with the same last name, are you related to her?" Well, it is an interesting question: Ellery Bicknell Crane in his 2 - volume set "The Cranes of Massachusetts" (pub. 1900) does a masterful job of tracing our family's ancestry back to the mid 17th century and to the immigration of a handful of Cranes who came to the New World. There were two brothers, Henry & Benjamin, and their father John Crane, who landed in Boston, and described themselves as being of "Muddy Brook" (generally the area around today's Boston University). The boys eventually moved once again to the Wethersfield colony on the Connecticut River. Another "Henry" Crane was located in the area of Milton, MA. He himself had a son and a grandson also named Benjamin, as if there might be some naming after, an uncle of ancestor, but there is at this time, no conclusive evidence.

Alexander Crane is descended from the Henry Crane of Milton, MA, I am descended from Benjamin Crane of Connecticut, son of John Crane, Muddy Brook or Boston, MA. If there is a connection it would be father of John and that would make Helen & myself eighth cousins, four times removed. But that matters little. The music is what matters and it is here and available, no longer sequestered away on a dusty library shelf. And the music speaks for itself.

           Bernard Crane
           arranger & editor   *January, 2019*

THE COMPOSER

Helen Cornelia Crane was born September 5, 1868, just a few short years after the end of the Civil War to Col. Alexander Baxter Crane, a native of Massachusetts and his young wife, Laura Cornelia Mitchell, a native of South Carolina. Col. Alexander Crane, a legal studies graduate of Amherst College was commissioned an officer on the side of the North and his young wife was daughter of the Wroughton Mitchell family of Charleston, South Carolina who for generations had lived in that part of the country. Certainly their relatives and acquaintances embraced both sides of the chasm that divided the nation. To this young couple was born Helen Cornelia, along with four other daughters and a son. Their earliest home was St. Mark's Place in New York's lower east side. Eventually Col. Crane's law career led to a flourishing Wall Street legal practice and they purchased property and built their permanent home in Scarsdale, NY.

She must have exhibited artistic talent at a young age since by her late teens she was embarked on studies in music in one of the most enviable of locations: Europe. She studied at the then "Klindworth-Scharwenka" Conservatory in Berlin. These studies culminated in her choice of composition as her major musical endeavor and she studied three years with noted composer and conservatory director Philipp Scharwenka. She was soon winning competitions and gaining much warranted recognition. German publishing houses recognized her work and she saw the publication of numerous of her pieces. Maintaining a regular home in Germany over the next couple of decades, she made several cross-Atlantic voyages for the sake of concertizing and teaching; one such trip in 1904 was for the purpose of hearing the Berlin Philharmonic perform her tone poem, *The Last Tournament* at the "World's Fair" that year, the *St. Louis Exposition*. She continued her intercontinental career until the fall of 1917 when the continued strife and turmoil of the First World War made it decidedly unsafe to continue.

At this time she returned to the her family home in Scarsdale, NY a place they affectionately nicknamed "Holmhurst" and here she remained for the most part; barring a few excursions & trip to Kaprun, Austria, where she traveled one last time "for the purpose of her health". Ultimately she passed away in November, 1930 in Scarsdale, NY and was laid to rest in the cemetery of St. James the Less Episcopal Church alongside her parents. She left behind her hand-written manuscripts in the care of her remaining siblings. Her youngest sister, Laura Vernon Crane Burgess ultimately donated this valuable trust to the New York Public Library, where the collection has been housed since the 1940's. Most of these pieces are there in their original manuscript form, showing the evolution of Ms. Crane's calligraphy and the blossoming of her musical art. Among this collection are over eighty works for the piano, several chamber works, orchestral tone poems such as *The Last Tournament*: her *Evangeline Overture, Cassandra* for female voice and orchestra, her *Serenade* for orchestra, two symphonies, *Psalm 42* for orchestra and chorus along with a multitude of song settings of various poets and pieces for organ. She was well noted in her day, lauded in various music periodicals of the time, even being listed in a compendium of composers in the United States, in *W.S.B Mathew's "A Popular History of The Art of Music..." (2nd edition 1906)*. But time is not always kind in its passing. Sometimes lives are dwarfed by events that overtake them in the memories of future generations. Bach was forgotten until Mendelssohn revived the memory of his music. And so it has been with Helen C. Crane. With this edition of her music hopefully our quiet sister speaks again. Let today's performers and today's listener be the judge. As a composer and as a music theorist, I do believe she warrants serious consideration. She stands as an integral part of the flowing forth of what is a truly "American" music, her life spanning that period of time between the Civil War and the "Great Depression", a time period known as the "Belle Époque", "the gilded age", a time shaken, rocked and irretrievably lost to an even greater war, World War I. Ms. Crane occupies a unique spot between late romanticism and the subsequent quest for new expression in music, enjoining her efforts to those of others, pushing the limits of tonality and yet retaining the memorable communication of which music is most capable.

Bernard Crane, editor
January 17, 2019

SELECTED ART SONGS OF

HELEN C. CRANE

MEDIUM VOICE

BOOK ONE

TABLE OF CONTENTS

I   Three Songs Op. 5

    1. Serenade text by Felicia Dorothea Hermans.. p. 1

    2. Sommernacht *(Summer Night)* text by Joanna Ambrosius Voigt............................p. 6

    3. Herbstlied *(Autumn Song)* text by Friedrich von Sallet......................................p.10

II   Four Lieder Op. 32   poems of Wilhelm Langewiesche

    1. Heimat *(Homeland)* p.14

    2. Morgenandacht *(Morning Prayer)* p.18

    3. Glücklich *(Happy)* p.21

    4. Erwarten *(Expect)*...p.24

III   Four Lieder Op. 34   poems of Wilhelm Langewiesche

    1. Mein Boot *(My Boat)*...p. 28

    2. Neues Glück *(New Luck)*...p.37

    3. Erkannt *(Recognized)*...p.46

    4. Winterwanderung *(Winter Wandering)* p.50

Serenade
for Mezzo-Soprano & Piano
No. 1

Helen C. Crane
Op.5, no.1

text is "Leave Me Not Yet" by Felicia Dorothea Hemans

©2020 Bernard R. Crane
all rights reserved

* if length of phrase is excessive, this is good spot to breathe

Helen C. Crane — Serenade — op.5, no.1

Sommernacht
for Mezzo-Soprano & Piano
No. 2

Helen C. Crane
Op.5, no.2

text from "Sommernacht" by Johanna Ambrosius Voigt

©2020 Bernard R. Crane
all rights reserved

Sommernacht

Helen C. Crane — Sommernacht — op. 5, no.2

TEXT & TRANSLATION

Sommernacht
   Johanna Ambrosius Voigt

Summer Night

Mit ausgespannten Armen
Kommt leis' die Nacht.
Drückt Feld und Wald und Fluren
Ans Herze sacht.

With outstretched arms
Comes quietly the night.
Pushes field and forest and corridors
Into its gentle heart.

Schlägt ihren weichen Mantel
Um Strauch und Baum,
Und summt mit Glockentönen
Die Welt in Traum.

Settles her soft coat
Around shrub and tree,
And hums with bell tones
The world into a dream.

Vergessen hat die Erde
Des Tages Weh,
Ich hebe meine Augen
Hinauf zur Höh'.

The earth has forgotten
Of the day,
I raise my eyes
Up to the heights.

Ein Vöglein seh' ich tauchen
Ins Abendgold,
Ach, wenn's auch meine Seele
Mitnehmen wollt'!

A bird I see diving
Into evening gold,
Oh, that my soul too
It might take with it!

Herbstlied
for Mezzo-Soprano & Piano

No. 3

Helen C. Crane
Op.5, no.3

text from "Herbstlied" by Friedrich von Sallet

©2020 Bernard R. Crane
all rights reserved

H.C. Crane — Herbstlied — Op.5, no.3

** though in the original m.s. the tempo is described as "Allegro ma non troppo", for text & note clarity the editor leans more towards the "non troppo"; more within the range of "andante"

TEXT & TRANSLATION

Herbstlied
    Friedrich Von Sallet

Durch die Wälder streif' ich munter,
Wenn der Wind die Stämme rüttelt
Und mit Rascheln bunt und bunter
Blatt auf Blatt herunterschüttelt.

Denn es träumt bei solchem Klange
Sich gar schön vom Frühlingshauche,
Von der Nachtigall Gesange
Und vom jungen Grün am Strauche.

Lustig schreit' ich durchs Gefilde,
Wo verdorrte Diesteln nicken;
Denk' an Maienröslein milde
Mit den morgenfrischen Blicken.

Nach dem Himmel schau' ich gerne,
Wenn ihn Wolken schwarz bedecken;
Denk' an tausend liebe Sterne,
Die dahinter sich verstecken.

Autumn Song

I walk through the woods,
When the wind shakes the trunks
And with rustling colored and colorful
Shake off leaf on leaf.

Because it dreams with such a sound
Beautiful from the spring breeze,
By the nightingale singing
And the young green on the bush.

Joyously, I scream through the field,
Where withered thistles nod;
Think of tiny mild May roses
With morning-fresh looks.

I like to go heavenward,
When clouds cover the heavens black;
Thinking of a thousand dear stars,
Who are hiding behind them..

Heimat

for Medium Voice & Piano

No. 1

Helen C. Crane

Op.32, no.1

text from "Heimat" by Wilhelm Langewiesche

©2020 Bernard R. Crane
all rights reserved

Heimat

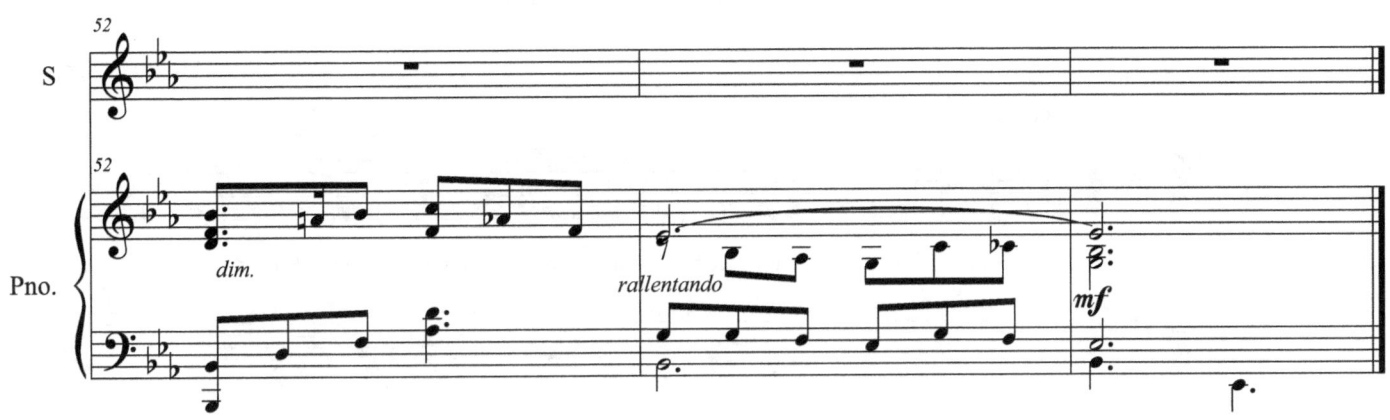

TEXT & TRANSLATION

Heimat
  Wilhelm Langewiesche

Heimat, ferne Heimat, du, die ich verließ,
Liegst vor mir im Traüme als ein Paradies.
Öffnest meiner Sehnsucht heimlich Tür und Tor,
Heimat, ferne Heimat, du, die ich verlor ...

Heimat, ferne Heimat, du, die ich verkannt,
Will ich Treue halten in dem fremden Land.
Aber meinen Kindern reife Korn und Wein,
Heimat, ferne Heimat, deiner Sonne Schein.

Home, distant home, you, whom I left,
Lie before me in the dream as a paradise.
Secretly open the door to my longing,
Home, distant home, you who I lost ...

Home, distant home, you who misunderstood
Will I keep faith in the foreign land.
But my children have ripe grain and wine,
Home, distant home, your sunshine.

Morgenandacht

for Medium Voice & Piano

No. 2

Helen C. Crane

Op.32, no.2

text from "Morgenandacht" by Wilhelm Langewiesche

©2020 Bernard R. Crane
all rights reserved

19

TEXT & TRANSLATION

Morgenandacht
   Wilhelm Langewiesche

Wenn in früher Morgenkühle
noch kein Fuss den Strand beschreitet
geh du still hinab und fühle
Wie die enge Brust sich weitet
Kniee dort im Sande nieder
Den die heil'ge Flut gereinigt,
Bis sich deine Seele wieder
mit dem Strom des Lebens einigt;
Bis in ihren tiefsten Ziefen
die versiegten Brunnen springen,
Und die Kräfte, die entschliefen
Sieghaft sich zum Lichte ringen.

Morning Prayer

When in early morning state of mind
no foot on the beach,
Do you go down quietly and feel
as the tight chest widens,
Kneel there in the sand,
who cleansed the holy flood,
until your soul returns
agree with the stream of life,
to their deepest depths
the dried wells jump,
and the powers that fell asleep,
victoriously wrestle in the light ....

Glücklich
for Medium Voice & Piano
No. 3

Helen C. Crane

Op.32, no.3

text from "Glücklich" by Wilhelm Langeweische

©2020 Bernard R. Crane
all rights reserved

TEXT & TRANSLATION

Glücklich
  Wilhelm Langewiesche

Samstagabendruh,
Meiner Woche Ziel,
gütig bietest du
mir der Freude viel:
Wellt dein Glockenklang
durch die Abendschein,
eine Stunde lang
darf ich glücklich sein.

Happy

Saturday evening rest,
my week goal,
kindly you offer me
much joy:
If your bells sound
through the evening light,
for an hour
I can be happy.

24

Erwarten

for Medium Voice & Piano

No. 4

Helen C. Crane

Op.32, no.4

text from "Erwarten" by Wilhelm Langewiesche

©2020 Bernard R. Crane
all rights reserved

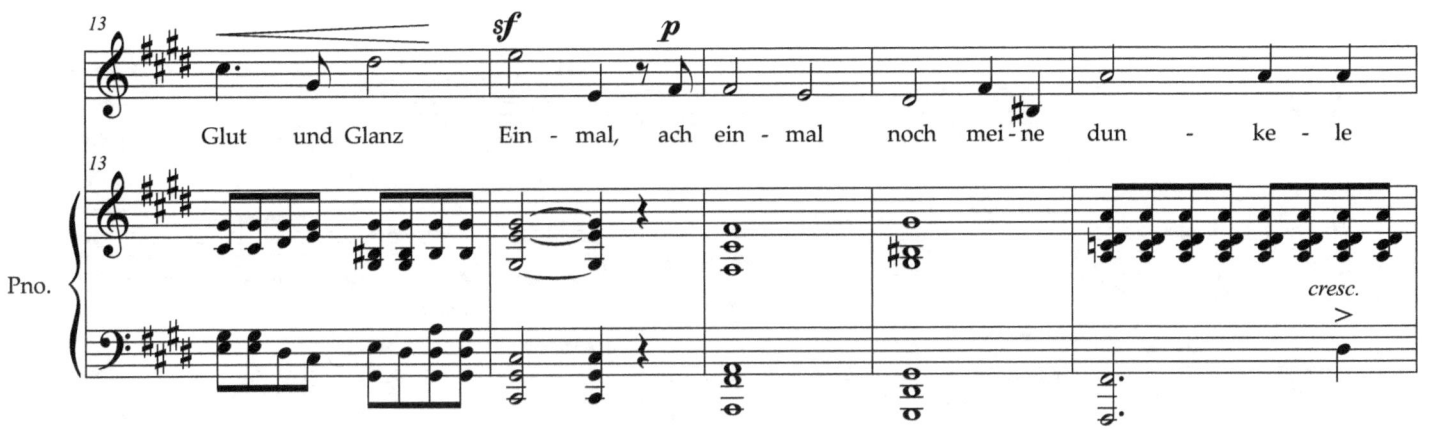

Helen C. Crane Erwarten op.32. no.4

TEXT & TRANSLATION

Erwarten
   Wilhelm Langewiesche

Liebe, du heilige, reine,
Fülle mit Glut und Glanz
Einmal, ach einmal noch meine
Dunkele Seele ganz,

Deren verlassener Garten,
Welkender Blätter voll,
Steht in bangem Erwarten
Dessen, das kommen soll....

Expect

You, love, holy, pure,
abundant with embers and shine.
One time, once more time
my dark soul made whole.

Their abandoned garden.
Full of withered leaves,
is in great expectation
of that which should come.

Mein Boot
for Medium Voice & Piano

No. 1

Helen C. Crane
Op.33, no.1

text from "Mein Boot" by Wilhelm Langewiesche

©2020 Bernard R. Crane
all rights reserved

Mein Boot

Mein Boot

Mein Boot

TEXT AND TRANSLATION

Es rauscht der Strom und zieht vorbei
Mit all den Nachen
voll Jubelsang and Lustgeschrei
voll Scherz und Lachen.

Wie lange nun erwart ich schon
Mein Boot vergebens,
Und führe doch zo gern davon
In Strom des Lebens.

Vielleicht, vielleicht kommt es erst an
In Abendgrauen....
O Seele wirst du gern dich dann
ihm anvertrauen?

Ganz sacht zerteilt zein dunkler Kiel
Die dunklen Wogen,
kein Wimpel ist dem Wind zum Spiel
emporgezogen.

Und nur die Sehnsucht steigt mit ein
und lachelt leise
und richtet deinen Blick
zum Schein der Sternenkreise

Und wenn sie müde wird an Bord
dann magst du schlafen:
Es weiss so gut der Schiffer dort
den Weg zum Hafen.

The current rushes and passes by
With all the boats.
Full of cheers and shouts of air
Full of jokes and laughter

How long do I expect now
My boat in vain
And feel free to lead away
In the stream of life.

Maybe, maybe it's just getting started
At dusk ...
O soul you will like yourself then
entrust him.

Very gently cut two dark keels
The dark waves
no pennant has the wind
drawn up to play

And only longing comes with it
and smiles softly
and directs your gaze
to the glow of starcircles

And when she gets tired on board
then you like to sleep.
The skipper there knows so well
The way to port.

Neues Glück
for Medium Voice & Piano

No. 2

Helen C. Crane
Op.33, no.2

©2020 Bernard R. Crane
all rights reserved

Neues Glück

Helen C. Crane — Neues Glück — op.33, no.2

44

Tempo I

Helen C. Crane — Neues Glück — op.33, no.2

TEXT AND TRANSLATION

Neues Glück
Wilhelm Langewiesche

In der stillen Nacht, wenn der Schlaf mich flieht,
Durch die Seele sacht eine Sehnsucht zieht.
Weckt mit Lebenshauch was ich lang verlor,
Lockt ein Hoffen auch aus dem grab hervor.
Seiner Einsamkeit, die so schmerzlich drückt,
Fühlt auf kurze Zeit sich das Herz entrückt.
Klingt ein Lied so weich wie ein Frauen mund
durch des Schweigensreich auf der Seele Grund.
Zieht das Tal entlang Lachen und Gelaut
Was im Herbst verklang, hat der Lenz erneut...
Hochzeitlich geschmückt träumt das weite Land.
Anemonen pflückt eine Mädchenhand.
Und ein weisses Kleid das im Winde weht,
Und ein Herz das weit für mich o-ffen steht.
Aus dem Heil'genschein den die Sonne flicht,
tief ins Glück
hinein schaut ein lieb Gesicht. Augen still und stet
leuchten mir herzein Wollen mir gebet und Erhörung sein.
In mein Leben schaümt neue reine Flut. Nichts,
noch nichts versaümt! Alles, alles, alles gut!
Herz nach langer Haft pochst du wieder frei
Schwillst in junger Kraft, ahnst Gnade sei..

New Happiness
Wilhelm Langewiesche

In the quiet night, when sleep escapes me,
Through the soul a longing pulls gently.
Awakens with life what I lost for a long time,
a hope lures out of the grave.
His loneliness, which squeezes so painfully,
feels for a short time the heart raptured.
Sounds a song as soft as a woman's mouth.
by the silence on the soul ground.
The valley draws along laughter and laughter
What had faded in the autumn, the Lenz has again ...
Adorned decorates the white land.
Anemones picks a girl hand.
And a white dress that blows in the wind,
And a heart that is wide open for me.
Out of the sanctity of the sun,
deep into happiness,
a sweet face looks. Eyes still and steady
light up my heart want to be prayerful and hear me.
In my life new pure floods are shining. Nothing,
nothing upsets! Everything, everything is good!
Heart after a long imprisonment, you pound again free
Swell in junior strength, divine Grace be

Erkannt

for Medium Voice & Piano

No. 3

Helen C. Crane

Op.33, no.3

©2020 Bernard R. Crane
all rights reserved

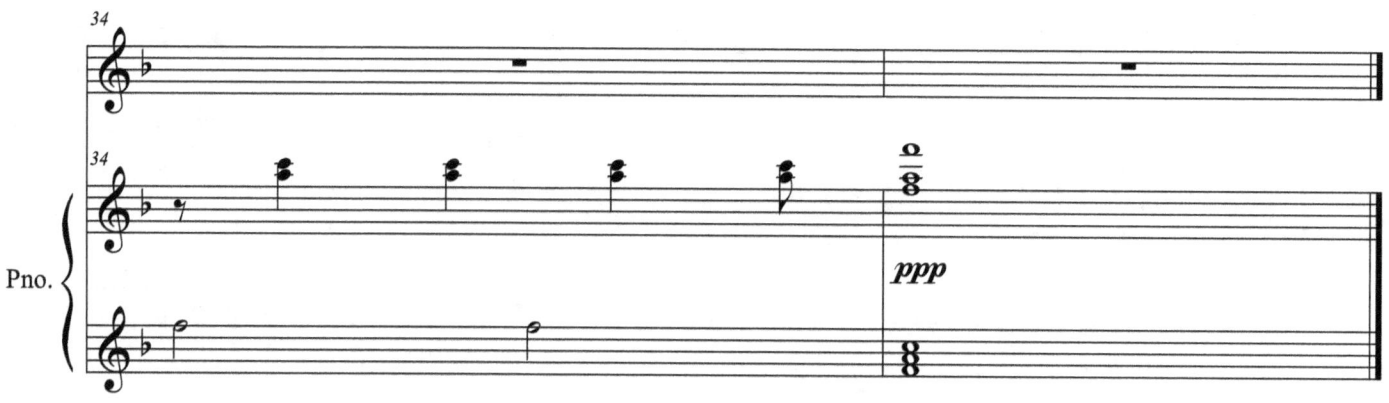

TEXT & TRANSLATION

ERKANNT
Wilhelm Langwiesche

Im Tale weitab lag die Stadt,
in einem hellen Schein,
durchs dunkle Land,
wie Silber matt aufleuchtend,
floss der Main
Und über Stadt und Fluss und Land
die nacht gewitterschwer
ein Sehnen, das sein Ziel erkannt
flog zitternd um uns her.

RECOGNIZED
Wilhelm Langewiesche

Far away in the valley lay the city,
in a bright light,
through the dark land,
like silver dimly glowing,
flowed the Main.
And over city and river and country
the night thunderstorm
a yearning, that recognized its destination
flew trembling around us.

Winterwanderung
for Medium Voice & Piano

No. 4

Helen C. Crane

Op.33, no.4

©2019 Bernard R. Crane
all rights reserved

TEXT & TRANSLATION

Winterwanderung
    W. Langewieche

Denkst du des Dezembertags:
Wie ein blauer schleier lag's
auf den Tälern, die verschneit
Ruhten und voll Müdigkeit.
Wie der Berge grosser Zug
Uns da in die Ferne trug,
Und den Lebensweg entlang
Vorwärts die Gedanken zwang!
Hinter uns die Kleine Stadt,
Dumpf und dunkel, träg und satt
Ein Geläute bang und schwer
Und vom Friedhof zu uns her
Sangen Sie und glaubten's nicht.
"Jesus meine Zuversicht".
Neben uns von Glanz umloht
Ging die Sonne in den Tod.
Aber vor uns Beiden lag
Ohne Ende unser Tag
Aber vor uns Beiden lag
Ohne Ende unser Tag.

Winder Wandering
    W. Langewieche

Do you think of the December day:
It was like a blue veil lain
on the valleys, the snow
Rested and full of fatigue.
Like the mountains big train
Carried us into the distance,
And along the way of life
Forwards thought forced!
Behind us the little town,
Dull and dark, sluggish and full
A laughter bang and hard
And from the cemetery to us
Sang and did not believe it.
" Jesus my confidence".
Next to us, surrounded by splendor
The sun went to its death.
But before us both lay
Without end our day
But before us both lay
Without end our day.